Finding
Gifts in
Everyday
Life

Best wishes,

Nancy Frey

Finding Gifts in Everyday Life

Nancy Coey

Cover Design and Illustrations
John Klingler

sweetwater press
Raleigh, North Carolina

Bookstore Distribution:
Login Publishers Consortium
800-626-4330

FINDING GIFTS IN EVERYDAY LIFE

Page Design and Layout: Jim Baxley, Artware

Publisher's Cataloging-in-Publication
Coey, Nancy B.
  Finding gifts in everyday life / Nancy Coey
  p. cm.
  Originally published: Bean dip and other stories.
  ISBN 0-9642515-1-5
  Preassigned LCCN: 94-67392
  1. Life. 2. Experience. 3. Parenting. 4. Expectation
(Philosophy)   I. Title.
BD431.C64 1995   128
                                      QBI95-20100

Printed in the United States of America

For Marcella Jordan Breen . . . Mom,
who had the gift of seeing, gently.

Foreword

You will laugh and you will cry reading this book. I know I did.

Nancy Coey has the uncanny ability to speak my words and express my joys and sorrows with more eloquence than I am able to give to my still voice within. Her honesty is endearing. Her humor is healing. Her tenderness is touching.

I met her fairly recently and knew immediately she and I would be friends forever. You will feel you have known her forever, too.

As you read her book and are introduced to her family and her circle of friends, and her dreams and ambitions and her foibles and fears, you will know that something very special has taken place between the covers of this book.

One woman, with eyes that see gently and a heart that remembers kindly, is about to share her personal recipe for looking at the world with Bean Dip eyes. (You'll know what that is all about as you read.)

And you will never again see those words that you will not think of this magnificent soul who can see the ordinary with such extraordinary spirit and, most importantly, can convey the wonder of it all to us with such great power.

This is a small book.
Because great truths do not need many words.
We understand immediately.
And are changed forever.

Rosita Perez
Author and Lecturer

Contents

Introduction

The idea for this book grew out of my teaching experience. For years as an instructor of the dreaded Freshman English, I wrestled with this question: How can a nineteen year-old from Micro, NC, a kid who hasn't been many places, and who hasn't seen very much, write a paper truly worth an A?

I finally figured out that the answer comes in three parts:

#1. Microcosm, the principle that underlies literature and makes it work, supplies the most important key. If you choose a small subject carefully enough and then talk about it with enough detail, you will end up talking about something large. Literature abounds with examples: Willy Loman, Hamlet; in fact, microcosm is true every time.

#2. If you define success as doing well what you set out to do, *set out to do a small task, then do it very well.* Almost like a painter hired to paint a cinder block wall with only a small hobby-size jar of paint. The fool will say, "Hey, I'll add water and do the whole job;" the one who'll be hired again will guarantee only one block. A freshman paper is only a small jar of paint. So is a book, and so is each day in our lives.

#3. There is a definite, set number of human emotions . . . maybe 37, maybe 426. But a definite, set number, and every one of us - throughout time - participates in these emotions. They do not change. They are the same for everyone. So, if you speak honestly, with enough detail, you touch the underlying common thread.

Through your life and through your stories, you not only can touch the bond that connects us to each other, but you even can make it stronger.

When our boys were little, their favorite stories began "Once upon a time a little boy named . . . ." Their faces would light up; their bodies would quiver with anticipation, then relax into near bonelessness as I would tell them about something wonderful they had done that day.

We all still need that. We need to hear our own stories, to "watch" ourselves as we lead our lives, to take delight in the joy, and to learn from the pain. Because "once upon a time" is now.

Every story in this book is true. They are all "small" but maybe not small at all. Because they make up a life. I hope they help put you in touch with your own stories. And that you find your own brand of bean dip.

Small Things

Bean Dip

When I got out of graduate school, I got my first teaching job at The University of Hawaii. I lived in Hawaii for five years and during that time a couple of really important things happened. One is that I met a handsome young Air Force Captain by the name of Donald Coey and my mother said, "Thank God!" She had been asking for years, "Can't you find anybody? Anybody at all?"

So that was really important.

But the second thing was almost as important. I made three wonderful friends: Fay, Marie, and Julynn, and the four of us would play bridge together. Since we were all poor, and none of us was even remotely interested in cooking, we had gotten into the habit of simply having chips and bean dip.

One day, Fay, who was from the South, happened to refer to us as "Sisters of the Lodge." We said, "Who?" "Sisters of what?", and made fun of the expression, but just as quickly adopted it. From then on, whenever a sister called to set up bridge, she would say, "I'm calling a Lodge meeting."

I want to tell you about our Lodge meetings. First of all, we hardly ever played bridge. On one memorable Saturday afternoon, we never even got out the cards. You see, we were all single in those days, and each dating men we would eventually marry, so we had a lot to talk about.

And it was important talk. I wouldn't be Nancy Coey today if the Lodge sisters had not approved of Donald Coey. They were friends, but more than friends; they were family, and their approval meant everything to me.

Well, Fay and Marie still live in Hawaii but Julynn, the center of us all, the heart and soul of the Lodge, my maid of honor, died of cancer nine years ago and cannot *ever* be replaced. The Lodge is over. The Lodge is finished. It will live forever in my heart, but it does not exist on earth anymore.

But, as Paul Harvey would say, the rest of the story is this: about two or three years ago, one of our kids did something very big and very bad. And, the truth is, I don't remember what it was, but at the time it was terrible to me. Now, I'm very emotional, but I hardly ever cry. My husband happened to call me at work that day, and I started to cry over the phone.

And I believe that he got very scared.

When I got home from work that evening, guess what was on the kitchen table? BEAN DIP!!! I hadn't seen a can of bean dip in twenty years. Do you know how far back he had to reach to find such comfort for me? And I thought to myself, "There are now just three other human beings alive on this planet who know the significance of bean dip. *How lucky I am because I am married to one of them!*"

I'm in the grocery store now, and I see that Frito-Lay Bean Dip; you know what I'm talking about - swoosh, you open the can, - and I think to myself, "That man of mine can do a lot wrong but I am married to him forever."

Because he saw it. I know you know what I mean.

The power of small things. Look for them in your life, and use their power to lift you up.

Sharing a Treasure

We're a few weeks into a Fundamentals of Speech course and a gentle, shy nineteen year old gets up to give her first speech. She is very nervous, and we all look down, wanting not to scare her. The room is quiet. We're not expecting very much, just hoping she'll get through it and not cry.

She starts to speak, and we are spellbound. She tells of working as a bus driver while in high school, of being assigned to a bad neighborhood, of kids who give her trouble from the first day.

In particular the worst one, a boy of about ten.

One winter day, there's a patch of ice on the road, and she needs to back up to get a running start. She can't see out of the rear window and asks for help: "Is it clear?" The boy says, "Yes. You can go." She backs up . . . and into a three foot ditch. A tow truck must be called; the principal arrives; she almost loses a job she badly needs.

But that's the low point; with each passing month, things improve. Finally, it's the last day of school. The boy is busy on the bus, going from seat to seat, but she overlooks it because he's been good for so long.

When they arrive at school, the kids are excited and all crowd around her. They know that today is also her birthday. The boy has gotten her a card, and everyone has signed it, and they are very proud as she opens it.

It is a *used* birthday card. The boy's name has been scratched out.

She has brought it with her to our speech class, and she holds it up for us to see. And we clap until our hands hurt.

We all know that we are seeing more than a card.

Excess

When I was a junior in college, I heard that a number of kids were going to Europe the next summer. I wanted to go very badly so I worked hard that year, saved $1100 and, in July of 1964, went with my friend Jeannie to Europe.

Now, thirty years later, one moment still stands out: We are in a big empty room in Versailles Palace. Empty, that is, except for a large THING in the middle of the floor. A beautiful thing. About four feet long, two feet wide, waist high, hollow, made of gold.

A GIGANTIC GOLDEN BOX!

Jeannie and I walk around it. "What do you think it is?"

We hang around until a tour group comes in. The guide says, "This elegant filigree piece was a wedding gift to Marie Antoinette from the citizens of Paris."

"What is it?", says a member of the group.

"Oh," the guide says, "it is a centerpiece for the dining room table."

At that moment, I understand the French Revolution.

The Chair

As our oldest prepared for his first out-of-state summer job, we rummaged through the attic to find pots, pans, and cooking utensils.

It brought back some long-ago memories. When we got our first unfurnished apartment, it was just that: unfurnished. We had a bed, elegant silver and china wedding gifts, and not much else.

And, of course, we had very little money.

We bought a chair at a garage sale for $35. And it sat, gorgeous but alone, in the living room. We'd move it from one side of the room to the other: "Does it look better *here* or *here*?"

We would *race* through the dishes because the first one finished would get the chair. And a whole lot of snuggling went on in that chair.

It's been recovered twice now and is a cherished part of our household. When our children start furnishing their own places, we'll help out where we can, but that chair is ours, and it will stay home.

Some things are not subject to negotiation.

What treasures are important to you?

The Turn-Around

A lady named Lena made a big difference in my life.

Here's how it happened.

We had been living in the D.C. area for all of two weeks when we were invited to a neighborhood get-together. A lady asks, "Well, how do you like it here so far?" I'm feeling lonesome and overwhelmed and decide to tell the truth. To take a risk!!! So I open my heart to a stranger and tell this story:

When I was growing up, Aunt Helen and Aunt Marcy would come for Thanksgiving and Christmas and they would always bring Russell Stover candy. Russell Stover candy became for me the symbol of good times, of special events; it was then, and is to this day, the treat-of-all-treats.

With that explained, I tell her that just today the kids and I went to a nearby large shopping mall for the first time. Scary; fancy stores that our old hometown didn't have. The boys loved it, but I was intimidated. Then I remembered Russell Stover candy. And Aunt Helen and Aunt Marcy who always seemed rich and sophisticated to me. So I said, "Boys, we're going to get ourselves a treat!" And we marched into Bloomingdales and headed right for the gourmet section. A very well-dressed clerk looked down at us and said in a tone that still hurts, "Bloomingdales doesn't carry Russell Stover candy. You might try the drugstore . . . ." Diminished, the boys and I left and went straight home.

I say all that, feel better just for the telling but, of course, she hears, "I'm not going to like living in a big city."

The party goes on; conversations ebb and flow; the evening ends. The next day, the doorbell rings.

It's Lena with a box of Russell Stover candy.

Things begin to look up.

Kindness

It's the middle of August and very, very hot. I'm driving back home from a speaking engagement. It's a six-hour drive and I'm exhausted. Not just from the drive, but from very little sleep the night before. Anticipating the talk, and unable to get the motel temperature right, I was awake most of the night.

Groggy and spacey, now. Driving in a fog.

Pull into a rest stop and head right for a soda. Fumble forever with the coin changer: first put the bill in upside down, then in the wrong direction. Finally get change, then stand in front of the drink machine and cannot figure out where the coins go. It's as if my battle with the coin changer has taken every last bit of mental energy I have. Tentatively move my arm once or twice toward the machine, then just stand, confused.

A voice says, "Here, ma'am, this is where the coins go." And a very large hand points to the spot. I look over and in front of me is the sort of person I usually ignore: diesel cap; large belly hanging over his belt; cigarette dangling from his lips. He sees my surprise - or fog - and says, almost contritely, "I

14

didn't mean to be smart, ma'am. It's just sometimes these machines can be tricky."

Yes, sometimes they can be.

And sometimes even putting one foot in front of the other can be tricky. And sometimes we are showered with kindness in unlikely places, in unlikely ways, by unlikely people.

Is there a lesson here?

A Chain of Small Events

We went on a vacation years ago to a lake place in northern Wisconsin. It was advertised as a "family resort," and indeed it was. Families stayed in rustic cabins scattered around the property, and three times a day a large iron bell would gong, signalling mealtime. The food was great; the college-age waiters and waitresses were friendly and energetic and, by the end of the first meal, we knew we would love the place.

But the best part was the daily activities. Every day had some contest: horseshoes, fishing, tennis; there was even a talent show on Friday night, and the guests were the talent! Everything was a competition, in a very friendly sort of way, and we were told that on the last night trophies would be awarded to the winners in each of the categories.

Just about everyone signed up for at least one activity. It didn't matter if you were any good or even if you knew the game. We played things we had never played before, with people who also had never played before.

And it was wonderful.

Finally awards night arrived, and people *beamed* as they walked to the stage for their trophies. Thunderous applause; trophy held high; modest words of appreciation and acknowledgement. It could have been the Academy Awards. Meanwhile, we were in a tiny place in the woods. The trophies were plastic, about six inches high. Cost, maybe, twenty five cents.

No matter. They were *important*. And I remember Awards Night and the pleasure on the faces of the lucky trophy winners.

Ten years later, I almost get my first trophy. I'm in Toastmasters; give my first speech and win "Speaker of the Day." I am given a small "Golden" trophy and triumphantly bring it home. Within minutes the phone rings, "Do you have the Toastmaster trophy?" "Well, er, yes." Long pause. "Well, that's a *rotating* trophy; it's given out at each meeting. No one is supposed to take it home; it belongs to the club." "Oh. Sorry. I thought it was mine. I'll return it."

A year later at the Toastmasters Awards Banquet, I receive the "Speaker of the Year" trophy, given to the person who has most often been "Speaker of the Day." I'm delighted and proud, but hold the prize gingerly; perhaps it must be given back.

Not so. It is permanent.

Mine. Forever.

Another year passes. I'm teaching a speech course and get the idea to incorporate "Speaker of the Day" and to use my Toastmasters trophy as the prize. The day's winner is *thrilled*; in accepting, she acknowledges people all the way back to her grandparents. The class is respectful and serious, and I'm thinking, "This idea is a winner." But, not only is the trophy small and rotating, it is small, rotating and has my name on it!

No matter.

Still precious. Coveted, even.

One young man takes it home for Thanksgiving, and his family is so proud they have him give his speech in front of all the relatives.

If you ever hear somone say that small things don't count, don't believe it. Small things count a lot.

Moments . . .

A Small Backyard

We moved to the Washington, D.C. area when the boys were about six and eight. The backyard was pretty small, but in the middle was a gigantic oak tree and right away I started dreaming about a treehouse. My husband, who is not very comfortable with tools, immediately protested. "How often do you think they'll use it? It'll be real popular for a short time, and then it will just sit."

Well, yes; I guess that's true . . . so I dropped the subject.

A few months later, I could still see the treehouse. I brought it up again. "How often do you think . . . ?"

Yes; you're right.

A year passed. I thought of it again and called a carpenter to come out and give me an estimate. He laughed at me. "Lady, I don't build treehouses."

I dropped it.

Another year passed. By now the oldest is close to eleven

and the time for treehouses is fast running out. I say to my husband, "About the treehouse . . ." But this time, when he starts to say, "They'll never use it" I interrupt and from my soul this comes, "*It's not for them. It's for me. I need to be the kind of mother who builds them a treehouse.*"

Things had changed.

We found Paul Wiles, a retired carpenter, who knew magic when he saw it, and who cared about that treehouse. After nailing in the last floorboard, Mr. Wiles stood on the platform he had just created and danced a jig of pure happiness.

I watched and clapped.
And then climbed up and danced with him.

Yes, the boys never did use the treehouse much. In fact, we moved less than a year later, and the new owners tore it down.

But we had the dance . . . and we have the memories.

After the Dance

About three weeks after the treehouse was finished, we got a call from Mr. Wiles' daughter. Mr. Wiles had been in a car accident, was in the hospital, and was in pretty bad shape.

The boys and I went to see him. A nurse was with him when we arrived and overheard us saying that we had brought pictures.

"Oh, great!", she said. "I want to see this famous treehouse."

He had *talked* about it.

When we left, the pictures were on the wall.

Who ever said that treehouses were just for kids?

Many Parts

I am sitting in Marie's kitchen early, early on a Tuesday morning. I arrived in Hawaii the night before to visit with our mutual, much-loved friend who is very sick. The long flight, the emotion of the visit, and the early morning, unfamiliar sounds of Hawaii have all awakened me long before my usual time.

Marie's roommate, a woman in her sixties, a schoolteacher retired in Hawaii and active in Common Cause and a dozen other community things, comes in and, after fixing her coffee, sits down across from me.

We are meeting for the first time but, within minutes, we're talking important talk . . . perhaps being in pajamas helps. Soon I say, in answer to "What do you do?", "Well, my children are young now, but eventually I want . . ." And immediately she hears it all: the love, certainly, but also the frustration and the impatience.

And she says, "Life is long and has many parts."

That happened twelve years ago.

Not a week has gone by since then that I have not thought, "Life is long and has many parts."

The trick is to know which part you're in now, and to be there fully. Easy to say, not always easy to do.

Especially if your heart is in Part Six and your life is in Part Five, or the other way around.

But worth working towards.

The Rockets' Red Glare

I would hardly describe myself as a sports fan but over the years, the only female in a male house, I have come to learn and appreciate.

And I think men are onto something!!!

If, for example, you've never been to a baseball game, you may just be missing out on one of life's real treasures. I confess that I have never watched two consecutive plays in any one game, but I sure have had hours of pleasure watching everything else.

In the minor leagues, for example, before a game young boys line the fence hoping for autographs from players who are their heroes. And the players all strut, fairly bursting with joy and pride and the dream of getting called up to the majors. And the summer night air is ripe with the hope of those dreams.

You can feel it.

Then comes "The Star-Spangled Banner." At our ballpark,

everybody sings, and a giant scoreboard flashes the words, so you can be confident about the tricky parts; (is it "war bombs" or "the bombs"?)

There are times, as we stand to sing, when I see my husband tall and proud and happy, and kids clutching autographed baseballs and wearing caps and holding pens and scorecards, and hear Dads whispering, "I'll explain a foul ball in a minute, son" and moms saying to one another, "Well, at least it's an evening out" that I think to myself, *it just doesn't get any better than this.*

And the game hasn't even started yet.

PLAYBALL!

A Secret You

Years and years ago, back when I was single and teaching at the University of Hawaii, I happened to see a notice in the school newspaper about tryouts for an upcoming production of Shakespeare's "Coriolanus."

Other than holding leaves in my hand, and sprouting branches from my head in second grade ("I think that I shall never see, a poem as lovely as a tree"), I had never been in a play. But that notice came at a tough, lonesome part in my life, and I needed something.

I chose a scene from "Romeo and Juliet" and for days practiced heartfelt feelings which I emoted, when the time came, across the tryout stage.

I gave myself chills.

But evidently not the director. When the casting list was posted, I was one of the "rabble," or hungry mob. We smudged our faces with dirt; dressed in rags; clutched the hems of noble garments, and cried out, "Bread! We need bread!"

Not exactly what I had had in mind.

But, glory of glories, the director gave me a line to say *all by myself!* I will remember it until I die: "You have received many wounds for your country." I practiced that line so many times, in so many ways, that when my friends called, instead of saying, "Hello," they would say, "You have received . . ."

Opening night came and I was told by a number of people that they had never heard a line spoken with such feeling. I sensed the sarcasm, bronzed my rags, and retired from the theater.

But some experiences sink deep. There will forever be a secret part of me that thinks, "We in the theater . . ."

Who lives inside you???

No Locks Needed

Don and I were married only a few weeks when we bought bikes at a garage sale.

They each cost $5.

But they worked great, and we were happy with them. The best part was that no matter where we left them and no matter how long we were gone, whenever we came back, we always found them in the same place.

Nobody ever messed with our $5 bikes!!!

A couple of years later, we bought brand new bikes and when we got them home we realized that now we needed locks. I remember thinking, "Is this what getting stuff is all about? As soon as you get it, do you have to start worrying about how to keep it?"

Now, many years later, I have a glimpse of the answer: could it be, ironically, that the most precious things of all are the

very things which need no locks to begin with? Health, free-
dom of choice, memories, moments, love???

Maybe the best things in life really are free?

It's Not Called Gilligan's

We had moved seven times in the first twelve married years and were determined that this transfer would be the last.

We bought a forever-house.

And then we did forever-things. Like putting up a basketball pole in the driveway and sinking it in concrete, and then pouring concrete inside the pole for added stability.

But that isn't the best part. You see, behind our house are woods, and at the very back of our property is a creek. Before getting curtains, drapes, or rugs, I made a path down to the creek. I raked and chopped and dragged fallen trees to line the way, then put large flower-filled tubs to signal the entrance to the path. And every spring I clear the path from the growth and damage that has occurred during the previous winter.

Why?

Because the path not only leads to the creek, it leads to a tiny island in the middle of the creek. And it's not called Gilligan's

Island. If you go there on a late summer afternoon, the ferns growing wild all around bathe you in their musty perfume, and the sun slants through the trees just the way the sun is supposed to slant through trees.

And if you sit in an exact, certain way, you have an illusion of total privacy because you cannot even see the house.

If you want to be there with a friend, you've got to be very clever because Coey Island is small. So small, in fact, that there's not room for two ordinary chairs; you need to have small, beach chairs . . . and then place them perfectly; otherwise one of you will be in the water.

But I promise you this: the time there is worth the effort.

What moments are important to you?

Everybody Needs
Somebody Sometime

Lonesome

A fellow teacher and I got an apartment along the Ala Wai Canal, right in the heart of Waikiki. Twenty-three years old, single, living in Honolulu. It couldn't get much better, right? But a tricky thing happened. After three months or so, when the initial excitement wore off, I started feeling the blues.

I didn't think that would happen in Hawaii.

One day, I walked down to the canal and sat along its banks to figure out what was wrong . . . and eventually I understood the problem: *lonesomeness*. But as I was sighing, crystal clear water flowed past, and the air was so clear that purple mountains, although far off, looked close enough to touch. I could not think of even one person who would want to hear a song of woe from someone in my circumstances.

No one would feel sorry for me.

Which, of course, made me feel worse. Because sharing my troubles with a friend had always been a sure-fire way to feel better. I knew folks back home would say: "Yeah, tough; I wish I had your troubles."

So, that's how I learned a big, big lesson: you can easily be miserable in a beautiful place.

Because the place doesn't have anything to do with happiness. People do.

Part of a Team

When Magic Johnson first announced his retirement from the NBA, he was asked, "What will you miss the most?"

He thought a moment, and his reply went something like this: "I'll miss all the things you would think I'd miss . . . the locker room, the games, the pressure, the sweat . . . but most of all, I'll miss the uniform. Because, without it, I'm Earvin Johnson but with it, I AM MAGIC!"

Nobody does it alone.

Who's on your team?

Hooked by a Smile

I'm at the grocery store: ordinary trip, nothing special to buy, just the basics. As I near the end of the aisle that empties at the meat counter, the butcher catches my eye and yells out, "You've come for the salmon."

I turn around; surely he's not talking to me. But there's nobody behind me.

The salmon?!? I'm thinking bread, milk, and maybe some hamburger.

"No," I say, and start to walk on.

"But it's on *special*," he says. "A great price."

I don't know what to do with salmon. I've never bought salmon. I've never even thought of buying salmon.

But there's something very appealing about this guy's voice - and about his smile. I like him. And I like that he has picked me out. He seems to know that I need salmon. So I walk over and order a pound. But I'm in a hurry, so I leave him to it and get on with my shopping.

When I get back, there is a *crowd* around the counter, five deep. I ask, "Are you all here for the salmon?"

Some look embarrassed, as if they, too, have gotten hooked, but all answer, "Yes. The salmon."

Later, at the checkout line, I wait for the manager; I cannot let this experience go unpraised. Then I go home and try to figure out how to cook salmon.

How often have you been hooked by a smile?

Topsy

The truth is, I've never much liked cats. I grew up with a gorgeous, loving dog and have always thought that cats were, at best, poor imitations. But I married a man who grew up with cats.

So we have a cat.

Here's what amazes me about her: she knows how to get what she needs. At the simplest level, she meows when her food dish is empty, stands at the door when she wants to go out, and heads right for her favorite spot in the sun when she feels like taking an afternoon nap. But what really amazes me is that she demands - and gets - love when she needs it. Sometimes, even if she has recently eaten, been outside, and had a nap, she'll still cry and rub up against somebody's leg, asking to be picked up.

She wants to be *loved*.

It's as if she is saying, "Hey, guys. Pay attention to me." And when she gets what she needs - a fill-up - she jumps down and goes her own, infuriatingly independent, cat way.

Why don't we learn from our pets? Why don't we say, "I'm feeling a little blue right now. I need a hug."

"If he really loved me he would know" is baloney.

Want to purr?!? Try talking next time.

A Special Place

I love my hair salon. No matter what's going on, when the time comes for that once-a-month-color-and-cut, I am ready.

For sure I like having my hair done, but I look forward to going mainly because the salon is such a happy place. There's anticipation and excitement and *hope* in the air because women are having fun and talking and telling secrets and looking better.

What is not to like?

It amazes me that I can feel so at a home in a place filled -let's tell the truth here - with things far outside of my comfort zone. Like magazines featuring gaunt models wearing skimpy clothes, and pictures on the walls of hairdos never seen in any of the grocery stores I go to.

But who cares? What's important is that all who work there are upbeat and good at their jobs; they make us look great, and they listen as we talk.

And talk we do.

The place buzzes.

As I sit with goop on my hair, I see women in every booth *leaning* into the reflected image in the mirror.

More than hair is getting fixed.

The Soup Pot

Family is important . . . but tricky, don't you think?

On the one hand, everybody needs a comfort place, a place that is home, where you can relax, and be yourself. Where you don't have to *pay*; where you can just *be*. A place, as Robert Frost suggests, that you do not need to deserve.

Yes.

Of course.

On the other hand, since family is so important, why do we often treat strangers better than we treat family? Why do we sometimes work so hard to be part of the group at work and then succumb to near negligence in being part of the family?

If you want to come home at the end of the day and find the soup pot full, you've got to - at least occasionally - put something into it.

Shi–Shi

Other than having children, I've been in the hospital only once: years ago in Hawaii I had a small mark removed from my lip. It wasn't much of an operation, but it was serious enough to require anesthetic. When I woke up, a Japanese nurse squeezed my hand, leaned over so that her face was close to mine, and said in the gentlest of ways, "Do you need to go shi-shi?"

The story is worth telling, I think, for two reasons: one, even though I had never before heard the term, "shi-shi," I knew immediately what it meant (don't you?) and, two, even though the incident occurred close to twenty-five years ago, I still remember her face, and still remember *exactly* what she said.

I did not need to go "shi-shi," by the way, but I sure did need comfort and kindness . . . and that's why the moment sank in so deeply.

Wouldn't it be wonderful if she could read this now and know how much her kindness meant?!?

47

Waiting . . .

Too Late

Our first house was truly ivy-covered. And all of 900 square feet. But it was ours and it was adorable. The tiny side yard was enclosed by a white picket fence, a fence I painted one summer as our first baby lay sleeping in his carriage.

Ahhh, what memories.

Everything about that house was cute and clever. Since space was at a premium, the previous owners had rigged up shelving on the inside of the basement door so, even though there was no room for a pantry, we had a pantry.

Same with the bathroom. Sure, there was only one, but it was located off a clever half-landing, with easy access both from the downstairs and the second floor.

A doll-house.

We lived in that doll-house for four years and at a neighborhood going-away party two days before we left, a neighbor said, "Your house is special. My husband says that when he walks home from the train and gets to your house, he always feels that he is *home.* It is a beacon for the neighborhood, and I know he's not the only one who feels that way because I have heard other people say the same thing."

Now, we liked hearing this because we loved our little house, but we heard it as we were leaving. After the house was no longer ours.

Why did she wait?

The Baby Outfit

When our first son was born, one of his gifts was an expensive velour warm-up suit . . . just about the cutest thing I had ever seen.

It even had a little hood.

He wore it once.

How come?

Because it was so-good-I-would-put-it-on-him-only-for-special-occasions.

And when the next special occasion finally came, *he had outgrown it.*

It's bad enough to store clothes away, saving them for a day that may never come. It is tragic to do so with dreams.

What are you saving?

No Job Too Small

We thought that our ship had come in. In the mailbox one day was this notice:

Tired of waiting to get things fixed?
Can't get people to come to do the work?
Do you think your fix-up job is too small?
If your answers are yes . . . we can make you a satisfied customer.

Well, our answers were *all yes*! We had been trying for months to get someone to pour a parking pad at the back of the drive-way.

I couldn't call fast enough.

In fact, I called for two weeks. "Maybe they're on vacation," we said. Finally, someone called back; they would come on Sunday to give us an estimate. We waited . . . and waited. I called again. "*Next* Sunday," they said.

We waited . . . and waited.

On Mother's Day, four months after the first phone call, a congenial, smiling man appeared at our door, and I thought of him as a Mother's Day surprise.

Completion of the small job was a Labor Day surprise.

Unless you are good at fixing things, you sure do need to get good at waiting.

First To Speak

Have you ever done anything like this? Wake up one morning feeling just a little bit sorry for yourself? Nothing really bad going on, just nothing really good either. Days and days of the same kind of stuff. And all of a sudden you feel sick of it. And start to think, "Poor me."

And most days you can shake it off and press on, but every once in a while you feel like giving in to it, almost as if you *want* to feel miserable.

I bet everybody has done that.

I know I have.

So at the pool last summer when I heard my neighbor's story, I knew exactly what she meant. She had decided that morning, on an I-feel-sorry-for-myself-whim, to see how many *real* friends she had. She packed her young children off to the pool, as she did every summer morning, but this day she decided not to speak to anyone first. She wanted to see who and how many would speak to *her.*

When I got to the pool, about 4 P.M., she was still waiting, and looking mighty glum.

Some social experiments just aren't worth the cost, are they?

A Beautiful Dress

I come from a family of savers. We all carefully unwrapped Christmas and birthday presents so that the paper could be used again. Some paper got recycled for years at our house. It was the same with string and rubber bands; in fact, just about anything that could get reused, did.

Mom was the Chief Saver, the Guardian. She was careful.

Later, when I was grown, it hurt that she couldn't let me give her presents. I once sent mom and dad tickets to the Metropolitan Opera to see "La Boheme" because they had never been, and because I knew they would love it. My mother called - proudly - to say, "Your father and I were able to turn in the tickets and get full price." After many similar attempts, I gave up.

But not completely.

After her stroke, as she lay dying, mom was still mom, and as careful about details as ever. She planned her funeral; she even had me get the phone book to be sure I had the right number for the undertaker. And she let me buy her a dress to be buried in. I brought it to her hospital bed, and we both took pleasure in its beauty. Gossamer, and soft, and tender ... and the same blue as her eyes.

Other than for her wedding – and for mine – it was the nicest dress she had ever owned.

Maybe you can be too careful.

When the Rules Change

I won a Mickey Mouse watch in a coloring contest sponsored by a local grocery store. I was in the sixth grade and the second place winner was in the first grade. No wonder I won. I had no artistic ability *whatsoever* but I sure could stay within those lines. And it gave me great pleasure to do so. It was satisfying.

But that doggedness has turned out to be something of a handicap in adult life. When change is on the horizon, my first inclination is to grip my crayon tighter, stick out my tongue in concentration, lean intently into the project, and color harder and more carefully.

But that doesn't work when the contest is over, or when the rules have changed. If there's trouble at work, or at home, it doesn't make much sense to keep doing what you've been doing - even doing it harder - in the hope that things will get better.

As uncomfortable as it is to do, sometimes we have to go outside the lines.

Right There!

We've just moved to Washington, D.C., and are getting to know the area. A neighbor and I decide to go to the Supreme Court. We don't really think we'll be able to get in, but we'll try, and when it doesn't work out, we'll spend the day at the Smithsonian.

From the very beginning, it's one of those magic days that you remember for the rest of your life. Traffic is surprisingly light all the way into the city, and we get to the Washington Mall at 9:29 to discover that parking is permitted starting at 9:30.

We park almost right in front of the Supreme Court building, and walk up the impressive front steps. A guard is at the door, and we prepare ourselves for, "Who are you? Where are your passes?" He says, "Good morning."

We pass through a metal detector, then ask, "Where is the Courtroom?" "Down that hall; make a left; the big door in front of you." We expect a crowd in front of the door or certainly, at least, another guard.

There is just the door.

It is unlocked.

We open it, and are in the chamber of the Supreme Court. Sitting about forty feet in front of us are the nine Supreme Court Justices.

Don't wait. Set out . . . it might just be a magic day.

Encouragement

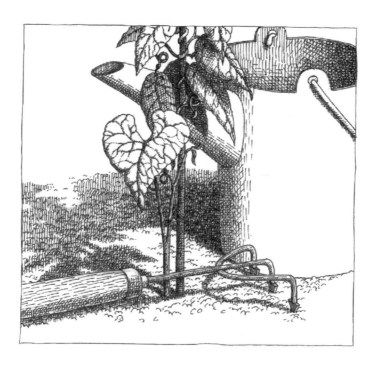

Take My Hand

Sometimes you come upon lessons in unusual places.

I learned about encouragement, for example, at an art gallery in Florence, Italy. Round a corner, and walk into the back room with me: standing free-form, all sides exposed, are the "Three Captives." Michelangelo had started to carve three David-like figures out of giant blocks of marble, but he didn't finish.

Viewed from the front, the figures lean forward, arms out-stretched; calf muscles rippling; weight on the balls of their feet. Walk to the back . . . the marble is untouched. These men are not leaning; they are straining.

They want to get out.

And we all want to help them. "Wait! Here, take my hand. We'll form a chain and, on three, we'll all pull."

That is what encouragement does . . . it lends a hand.

Encouragement helps people get unstuck.

Climbing to the Top

Our neighbors have a five year old, and when she was two or so, she was out at the hill by her mailbox. Well, not a hill, actually, more like a bump.

She would run to the top - even with her little stride, it was only about five steps - and her mother would clap. She'd stand at the summit for a moment, exultantly, then run down and do it again.

And her mother would clap.

This went on for quite some time. Eventually mom resumed her yardwork, but the little girl kept right on climbing.

Only now she clapped for herself.

What a nice idea: when we need it, to clap for ourselves.

Mowtown

My husband loves his lawnmower. We've had it longer than we've had kids, and the boys complain to their friends, "I've got to mow the grass with a lawnmower that is older than I am!" And their friends are astonished and feel sorry for them.

There has been so much grumbling in our house about that lawnmower that it has almost achieved the status of legend. So it was serious this past summer when it stopped working. Don was worried. But then he found Mowtown. And hope surged; a repair shop with a name like that would have to be good, right?

And it was. A week later the Lawnboy was back in its old form. And Don was a happy man. He called the Mowtown folks and from his heart said, "I gave you a sick puppy, and you gave me back a *tiger.*"

Who's keeping the legends alive at your house?

Never a Discouraging Word

A few years ago, one of our sons helped coach the Warriors, a boys' soccer team. A young team: ages six and seven. Our son would tell funny, painful stories of mishap after mishap: of boys kicking the ball in the wrong direction; playing in the dirt instead of playing defense. He was worried that they would lose all their games. "Don't worry," we said; "they'll be playing other six year olds. They'll do fine."

But he was right. They were awful, and they did lose all their games.

Towards the end of the season I'm chatting with a young father who's also waiting for practice at the various fields to be over: "How's the season going?", I ask. "Oh, fine," he says. "Last year was tough, but this year looks better." "Really?" "Oh, yes. The boys are maturing, and getting stronger all the time." "Is that right?" "Indeed. They almost scored last week . . ."

Later, as my son and I are driving home, he says, "Mom, why were you talking to Brad's Dad?"

"That was Brad's Dad?!? You mean we were talking about the infamous Warriors?!?"

Hats off to parents who always keep hope alive.

Get the Camera!

When our youngest was about seven, he was riding his bike on a Saturday morning. Earlier that morning it had rained very heavily and the ground was wet, muddy . . . and very slippery.

He was riding his bike way, way, way too fast. He slipped on an embankment close to a creek, sailed over the handlebars, flew twelve feet in the air, and landed in the creek. He walked two blocks home and when our older son saw him he yelled, "Mom! Dad! Come quick! Come quick!" We both ran out, and I will remember the moment until I die: He was *caked* in mud, eyes absolutely on the verge of tears.

Arms outstretched; my face contorted with pain, I said, "Ohhh, my baby . . ." My husband, at the same moment, started to laugh and yelled, "Get the camera!" *The mud cracked.* White teeth displayed themselves. He laughed. Then we all laughed. And took the picture.

We always have a choice, don't we?

The Work Itself

I once heard that "character is doing your work even after the mood is gone."

What a gold mine.

Because some days the mood *is* gone, isn't it? Some days trouble or worry clouds our minds. Or we don't feel well. Or we rather be somewhere else. And there's no one around to encourage us, and we feel too depleted to encourage ourselves.

That's where character comes in.

And something else happens, something almost magical: the work takes over and becomes its own reward. And then, at the end of the day, we can pick up our troubles again - chances are, they will be waiting for us - but, at least, we have done the work and accomplished something.

And we will stand taller.

When you don't feel like it, work anyway.

71

There's a Whole Lot of Good Going On

I find this ironic: I am a motivational speaker, but when I am asked to give a talk and call to interview a few of the people who will be in the audience, most times it ends up that *they* motivate *me*.

This is especially true with those in nurturing professions such as teaching or social work. When I ask teachers what they like most about their jobs, the overwhelmingly most frequent answer is "the opportunity to see children learn." And they go on to talk of challenges that are almost hard to believe: of children who have never seen a dog . . . or even an orange. Of children who hunger for love and affection; of children who cling to their legs and who don't want to go home to whatever horrors await them there.

I think of the social worker who goes into drug-infested projects to teach nutrition and healthful, economical buying habits to young mothers. I ask, "Aren't you afraid?" And she answers, "Honey, I've been in some scary places but with the help of the Lord, I always come out!"

And she's been doing this for thirty-three years.

I think of the judge in child-support court who answers the question, "What about your job gives you the most joy?" this way: "There is no joy in child support." And yet, when I ask if she would do it again, she answers, "Yes." Why? "Because it's a job that needs to be done, and there's satisfaction in seeing a big chunk of money being turned over."

She's catching bad guys.

The media is filled with news about the bad guys, but it rarely profiles the good ones. I talk to good guys all the time, and sometimes what they say leaves me breathless. And then I cannot wait to encourage them to keep on keeping on, and the circle completes itself.

We sure do need one another.

Parenting

The Truth, the Whole Truth

Do you sometimes suspect that parents exaggerate a bit about their children's achievements?

And it starts early.

In pre-school, when the children were tested for kindergarten-readiness, everybody I heard about was ready. Even the ones who were coloring on walls and torturing their classmates. And we were all too polite to say: *"You have got to be kidding!"*

Later, in middle school, one mother told me that her child learned all the capitals and all the presidents in two days while home sick. Whenever ours were sick, they watched "The Price Is Right!"

In high school everybody's children had high SAT scores. Did we have the only child in America who couldn't go to the Ivy League school of his choice?

No wonder raising the second child is easier.

You filter more.

Dashed

I have always secretly feared that I would be the only parent who wouldn't come through for the school play. And Dasher made the nightmare come true. He was the reindeer who did me in.

When our youngest was in the second grade, as luck would have it, he was chosen for the Christmas play. At first I thought, easy enough: the school supplied the horns, and I found a brown shirt. But, can we talk here?!? *There was not one pair of brown pants in our town.*

The teacher said, "Just dye a pair of old pants." "Just?" After ruining two pairs of pants, and one garbage can, I admitted defeat.

It was easy to spot Dasher: he was the reindeer in grey pants.

If you have to do "just" one more thing, stay calm . . . the show will go on.

Grandma's Advice

We were at a loss for words when he got his third speeding ticket. We had handled the first with a nice mixture of understanding and discipline; the second with discipline and threats of unimaginable consequences if there were to be yet another repeat. And here we were on a Friday night: a letter from the Highway Department burning our hands.

Only one thing was clear: we needed space . . . and time to talk. We went, just the two of us, to a nearby cafeteria. The place was crowded and even though we planned to save discussion until we were seated, it boiled up out of us as we snaked our way along the line. The positions were:
Me: "I'm sure he didn't mean to do it . . . maybe we should give him one more chance."
My husband: "Let him go to jail."

A little ole grandmother behind us couldn't stand it anymore: "Excuse me. I couldn't help overhearing."

"Let him fry."

A Self-Important Mother

I'm on a flight with thirty ten year old girls in red and white uniforms, and at least that many parents. They have won a State cheerleading contest, are on their way to compete in the nationals, and have taken over the plane, visiting and chatting. They are so excited - and so loud - that it isn't long before the rest of us begin to root for their competition. There is much switching of seats, and soon the girl beside me decides to be with her friend, and the friend's mother takes her place. This mother is very important. She is the trip's organizer and she talks, loudly, about how much work it has been.

Many details.

Then she begins to worry that daughter has not taken her medicine. Parading girls are told, "Get me my purse. Get me my purse." Finally someone listens; mother gets her purse. The next project is to get the medicine to daughter. "It is time for her medicine" is said more than once. Daughter, who apparently has been avoiding mother, finally appears. "Mom, I already took my medicine." "When did you take it? At the right time?" "At precisely the right time." "But did you take the right one... the yellow pill?" "Yes, Mom. The yellow pill."

Yes! My heart leaps in admiration, and I silently wish the girl well in what is likely to be a long struggle for independence. Mother, meanwhile, mumbles to herself, her importance momentarily diminished.

Suddenly, I hope the girls win.

Do controlling people bother you too?

For God and Country

Cub Scouts and Boy Scouts were big-time sources of stress.

You see, I don't know how to sew. I don't even want to know how to sew. When our son would go off to a Cub Scout meeting, I would say, "Please. If you love your mother, do not earn a badge." And he would come home proudly waving four of them, flashing that seven year old's toothless grin.

It was awful.

In time, he earned so many patches and insignias that he looked like a five star general. His uniform shirt was heavy with their weight; stiff and unbending, it was hard even to put on. But majestic and magnificent.

On the outside, that is.

The inside made the Los Angeles Freeway look like a country lane. Great highways of thread criss-crossing in a maze. Spots of dried blood. Faint echoes of imprecations muttered through clenched teeth.

Those proud mementos of past achievements now lie in the attic, preserved in state. They tell two stories: one on the outside, and one on the inside.

What trophies of yours belong in the "Parents' Hall of Fame"?

A Beacon

What are those words parents use when they want to tell you that it was tough, but when they don't want to be too negative or totally ignore that there was an awful lot of good or tell you too much about at times how tough it was? Challenging? Stimulating? Opportunities for growth?

All these apply. But, as a beacon for all of you with teenagers, I want to tell you about a recent trip to visit our college son.

Magical.

We see a basketball game, and it is as delightful as I thought it would be. We walk the campus, and it is even better. He shouts across the yard, "Hey, these are my parents." And he is talking about the very same people who were dog-meat only a year ago.

We smile and wave.

Then dinner with his darling girlfriend; everyone tender and careful and respectful of one another. Everyone clearly wanting this evening to be perfect.

And it is.

Later, as we drive home, I say, "Could we stop and get one of those vacuum sealed bottles . . . the kind they put ships in?"

I need to seal this day.

We Thought
We'd Never Hear It

We kept waiting all through those early years for signs that our sons loved one another.

While we encouraged them to pursue their own interests, and to have their own friends, we were careful always to have special family times: day trips; vacations; games of hide-and-seek in a darkened house; endless rounds of "Go Fish" and Monopoly.

We were fine when all four of us were together, but they never showed any interest in being alone together. In fact, just the opposite. When the oldest went to Boy Scout camp, packed in his bag was a prestamped, addressed envelope with the salutation of the letter already printed. When it arrived, it looked like this: Dear Mom, Dad, and XXXXXX,

So much for brotherly love.

A few years later my husband and I were in our front yard when through the window we saw them shoving each other. We ran in, just in time to see a livingroom chair get pushed so violently that it made a hole in the drywall.

You can still see the patched spot.

So it came as quite a surprise a few weeks ago when our college son said that he would come home to see his brother in a school play. "Yeah, right," we thought, certain that as the time got closer other, more important, things would interfere.

But, sure enough, he came and, after the play, they *hugged*. And the college man invited his brother to spend the night in his dorm.

We waved as they drove off. I could hear a chorus in the air: "They love one another. They love one another. They . . ."

We had waited a lot of years to hear that music.

Unrealistic
Expectations

Waiting for Something Wonderful

I'm sixteen, a junior in high school, and very strongly influenced by the great romantic novels I have read. My latest "Most Important Book" is <u>Jane Eyre</u>. I am in the garden with Jane when Mr. Rochester finally declares himself and wish for someone to say to me what he has said to her. Something like: "There is a string around my heart, the other end of which is attached to a similar part of your anatomy, so that whenever you move, I feel this curious tug."

Yes. That is what I wait for.

Finally, I think my ship has come in. Handsome A. J. Clark has invited me to his Junior Prom. At a hotel. Dinner first. Then dancing.

Yes.

As a memento, each young woman is given a cuddly panda with a card around its neck. It is on the table in front of us and, after dinner, A. J. Clark says, "May I write on the card?"

My heart stops. "Yes," I say, breathlessly. As he writes, I turn away. I cannot look. It is too wonderful.

Later, when he is gone for a moment, I read the card.

He has written my name. I turn the card over; then search every part of that panda. Surely there is more. No. That is it . . . *only my name.*

I do not remember the rest of the evening and never see handsome A. J. Clark again.

Have you ever ignored the good that is real because you're hoping for something more? . . . and isn't it always a mistake?

An Incorrect Assumption

We decide to get a cat. A long-haired cat. Within a few hours of getting it home, I seem to have developed a cold. Sneezing constantly. Then my eyes start to itch. I can't figure it out; strangest cold I've ever had. The next day, the pattern starts all over again. Finally I realize that I must be allergic to the cat.

But this is a very cute cat. We want to keep it. So I ask the vet if the cat can be given something . . . a shot?, some medicine? And he says, "Why? There's nothing wrong with the cat."

Sometimes the truth hurts.

One Perfect Day

We planned our wedding as if it were the Normandy invasion. We were determined that everything would be perfect.

The wedding took place in a small beautiful old church in Honolulu, and the reception in a military club on the slopes of Diamond Head.

Perfect.

We had friends who had been married in a very large wedding only a few months before, and they offered to help us prepare. We had diagrams; seating charts; maps for the out-of-town guests. Nothing was left to chance.

And all went off according to plan.

I was curious, though, on the receiving line, when the first guest mentioned shoes. Then another reference to shoes. "What's going on?" Don's rented tux came with shoes. As he knelt at the altar, everyone could easily read "10 1/2" written in chalk on his soles.

Jokes about that chalk were one of the highlights of our wedding, and I learned this:

Perfect is boring.

Chivalry

I'm in college and a bunch of us, sorority sisters all, are on our way to a party. All of a sudden, Anita, who is driving, says, "I think there's something wrong with the car." Fortunately, there's an on-ramp just ahead, so she pulls the car off the highway and onto the strip of grass alongside the ramp.

None of us know anything about cars, so we raise the hood to signal for help. Less than a minute later, a car slows down and stops next to us. Two young men. Perfect, we think; they will help us.

The driver leans out and says, "Is this the way to the Whitestone Bridge?" "Yes," we say. Armed with our answer, *they speed away.*

I can picture that moment now as clearly as when it happened.

And I am still astonished.

Pride Goeth Before a Fall

Sometimes you just have to be yourself because if you get too-big-for-your-britches-you-may-just-fall-flat-on-your-face. Case in point: my graduate school roommate, who had a great sense of style, took me in hand to ready me for a visit home. I was being met at the airport by a potential suitor, an older, sophisticated man, and the plan was: dress for success.

I stepped off the plane in a lime green coat, blue and green scarf, blue gloves, hose, shoes, and bag. The crowning touch: a pillbox hat. I was impressed with myself and as I walked toward the escalators I caught my reflection, more than once, in passing windows. I did look good. Head up, shoulders back, I stepped onto the escalator. I had meant to go down but the escalator was going up.

Do you know what happens when you step onto the top part of an escalator that is going up??? You fall down.

What do you think? . . . maybe dressing for success is not for everyone.

Another Babe Ruth

It's early June, and we hurry through dinner to get to the game in plenty of time. We set up our folding chairs on a hill, under the shade of a giant oak tree. A gentle breeze cools the steamy day into a soft summer evening. Off in the distance, our older son perches high in a tree, his spot for the game. Below us, the eight year old ball players are warming up. In their yellow caps, they look like a sea of ducks. Our eight year old has a baseball glove sticking out of his back pocket. He has gotten it by sending in chewing gum wrappers, and he is very proud.

We notice the coach scanning the crowd; clearly he is looking for someone's parents. I am suddenly sure that he is looking for us and equally sure that when he sees us, he will say either "Your son has the makings of another Babe Ruth" or "Your son seems to have only average ability, but I have *never* seen anyone with a finer attitude."

My instincts are right. He *does* approach us.

He says: "Do you remember after last week's game how the team lined up to shake hands with our opponents?"

"Yes. Yes," we say, eager for him to get to the good stuff.

"Well, your son was spitting at the other team."

The Flower Garden

Somewhere deep in my subconscious is this image: Victorian lady wearing large straw hat, rimmed with ribbon, strolling through manicured gardens, flower basket and small scissors in her hand. In a desultory and thoroughly delightful fashion, she collects flowers for the manorhouse.

She doesn't have a watering can, of course, because this Victorian woman does no real work, but somewhere mixed in this picture is a watering can . . . a childhood image, picked up who knows where, of green grass and sunshine and singing birds.

So once we were settled in our new house, I went out and bought leather-handled gardening tools, a large watering can . . . and a ribbon-rimmed straw hat.

Heaven.

But the *reality* is this: the tools are gorgeous, but ineffective for all but the smallest jobs; the watering can is so large and heavy that it is difficult to carry even when empty and, of course, next to impossible to lift if it has any water in it, and the stunning straw hat has gone to its final resting place since within minutes in the hot sun it caused my head to sweat so profusely that I could barely breathe.

And yet the image persists.

Why?

Bad Stuff:
Mistakes and Fear

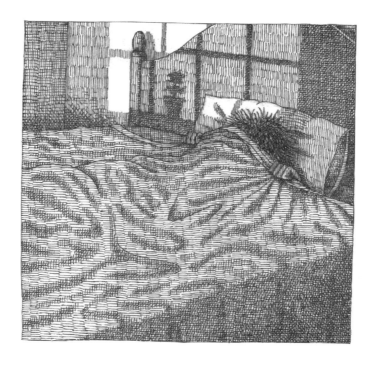

If I Had It to Do Over

He's in the seventh grade, has just made the varsity football team and struts around the house, posing in his uniform. He says things like, "Me hungry. Me need food." And we call him, "Bubba." Meanwhile, he's no real Bubba; he's third-string, and a gentle kind of kid, so this is all fun. But he does love being part of that team.

Unfortunately, he's strutting too much, and studying too little. One grade is especially bad, and we say, "If you do not pass English this quarter, no more football." Sure enough, he does not pass. Heartbroken, he resigns from the team.

You can touch the sadness in our house.

I step in for the first time now and discover that he knows very little about how sentences work, so we begin studying together every night. Soon he can pick out parts of sentences from fifty yards, in the dark, with his eyes closed and he and I both look forward to the next test.

His head is low to the ground as he brings home the grade. Not only is it another F, it is a deep F: 33/100.

I am very angry, and shout, "How is this possible?" Then I see the problem. The teacher gives a zero every time any part of an answer is wrong. And because he does not yet understand prepositional phrases, he gets a zero any time a sentence contains a phrase.

As hard as this is to believe, this teacher has ignored all that he has gotten right. Verbs; adjectives; adverbs . . . none of them count. She has erected a cathedral around prepositional phrases. I think, "What an idiotic way to grade," and suddenly understand the first quarter "F": the grading has been this rigid all semester.

But our son has quit the football team. And now the season is over. It is too late.

Talk about regret. If I had it to do over, I would have gotten the picture sooner and "Bubba" would have played football.

Have you ever made a mistake like that?

Smallness

Every once in awhile you come across someone mean, don't you? Not desperado kind of mean, but small kind of mean. Untrustworthy. Lover of gossip.

I knew someone like that. He was famous in our circle because he once told a secret to my friend Marie but before he told her, he made her promise not to tell anyone. This secret was really *secret*. Then he proceeded to tell her the very same secret that he had told her the day before.

He told the same secret twice to the same person. Every time we thought of it, Marie and I would laugh until we hurt.

Then we heard that he had gotten a dog. And we were surprised because he did not seem like the type. But then we understood. He was overheard bragging: he had gotten the dog *on sale*.

The poor dog . . . bought because he was a good deal.

Have you come to believe this too? . . . smallness is always a mistake.

A Special Parking Sticker

We sometimes handicap ourselves . . . and usually we even know when we're doing it. We say to ourselves, "Oh, I would never be able to do that!" And then it's no surprise when we can't. A self-fulfilling prophecy.

We have all seen it at work.

But I have never seen anything like this: a few years ago, an Egyptian student was in my summer school speech class. On the first day he waited to see me and said, "I have an accent and am worried that it will hurt my grade." I assured him that we would not penalize him for the place of his birth. If he did the work, he would have as much chance of getting an A as anyone else.

The next day he said more or less the same thing. And I gave him the same answer. The third time he mentioned his "problem" I began to feel uneasy. Why would he not accept an easy, truthful, happy solution?

His first speech revealed the answer: he was wedded to his problem. He told us that he thought he was "handicapped" because he was a foreign student, so he had been parking in the school's "Handicapped Zone." He asked the class' advice about how to handle all his parking tickets.

With so many citations, he now felt discriminated against and had even managed to construct what was probably for him the happy dilemma of seeing his problems multiply. With behavior like this, he might soon really *be* handicapped.

Sometimes we are, indeed, our own worst enemies.

Chicken of the Sea

Are there some areas in your life, some emotions or reactions, that just aren't rational? And people can tell you that it makes no sense to feel that way or that there is no reason to be afraid, and yet you still are?

Have you lived with a certain fear for so long that it has simply become part of who you are?

I'm that way about water. I don't know how to swim. I tried, once, when I was in my twenties to learn and took a course called, "Chicken of the Sea." On the last night we had to jump into the deep end of the pool, open our eyes, and tell the instructor how many fingers he was holding up. *I did it!!!* But then shook with fear at the memory of it and haven't had my head under water since.

So much for overcoming fear.

I go to the neighborhood pool in the summer only to socialize and get wet only to cool off. I know many three and four year olds because I hang out with those just graduating from the baby pool, the ones who spend a transitional summer at the shallow end of the big pool. I make new friends every summer; my old buddies no longer have time for me because they are too busy diving off the board and playing in the deep end.

Does fear make you an observer and not a participant?

Let's talk about it.

You can find me in the corner of the pool . . . down at the shallow end.

Too Close to See Clearly

Sometimes our friends hurt us the most.

Why?

Because they know us so well or, more precisely, they know the person we are *now* so well, that they cannot see the person we are capable of *becoming*. So, in ways subtle and unsubtle, they send the message: stay the way you are. And, then, the threat of loneliness gets added to the fear of growth.

If you want to talk about your dreams, strangers sometimes make the best listeners.

Trouble at Home

I'm distracted at a soccer game because I see that fool son of ours running down the field with his shoelaces untied. I want to yell, but don't dare; he would be too embarrassed in front of his friends. Just then a mother behind me yells, "John, tie your shoelaces!!!"

I can't believe it. I haven't noticed John's laces. But I sure have noticed our son's. And I bet I'm the only one who has.

College, the Army, the Foreign Legion . . . all these will be easy if children can only survive their *mothers*.

Mothers often see too much.

A little blindness goes a long way.

Saddle Up Anyway

I know people who are no longer ever afraid. They have gone through tough times and have earned belief in themselves. "Fear" is just a word for them, not a harmful, debilitating reality. I envy such people and hope to feel that way someday. But right now, for me, fear is still very real.

And pretty new because I never thought much about it until I quit my teaching job and went into full-time speaking. I had taken security for granted. I had taken self-esteem for granted. I didn't realize that I had been in a very self-contained, comfortable environment all my adult life, and that it would not be the same in the "outside" world.

And it wasn't.

For starters, people did not return my phone calls. And they didn't seem to think that a "motivational speaker" was much of a big deal. Or that I was necessarily any good. And I didn't know how to say, "Well, listen, pal; I am *real*." I would get angry. And depressed. But, mainly, I would get scared.

I remember - at my lowest - sitting out on the porch, mid-

July, my second month in business for myself. I began to think of the job I loved and had given up. I began to think of months stretched out in front of me of calling people who did not care about me. Of having time on my hands. Of doubting the dream.

And the fear was so real it was a physical pain. I moaned, aloud.

Now, most days I walk tall because I see the dream becoming a reality. How did it happen? No magic. No tricks. Basic stuff like keeping my head down when the way was toughest and not giving up. Learning from others. And one of the most helpful things I have learned is this: *Courage is not the absence of fear. Courage is going forward in the presence of fear.*

Perhaps you might cherish this John Wayne quotation as much as I do: "Courage is *not* not having fear. It's saddling up anyway and riding out."

Go get 'em, cowboy.

Words:
Sticks and Stones

The Power of Words

Words reflect reality. You see the dog; he is there. Then you say the word, "dog." Words reflect reality.

But they also create reality or, at least, change it. You love someone. That is a fact, a reality. But you have never said it. Then you say it. And the reality is changed.

Words are precious and precise and powerful.

And words count a lot.

Scorched

My friend tells this story about her two year old son:

He is very, very angry at her. Evidently she has offended him in some way and he wants to let her know just how mad he is. But he is having trouble because he knows very few words . . . maybe twenty or so. He scrunches up his face; thrusts his head, turtle-like, from his neck, and seethes, *"You, you . . ."*

But then he gets stuck.

He doesn't have a word for what he wants to say. You can see him thinking, making choices.

Finally he has it: *"You, you . . . firetruck!"*

His mother jumps back, scorched.

Words can sometimes burn.

I'll Send Candy

I call to send Grandma flowers for Mother's Day. The telephone operator has a strong big city accent and a very impersonal tone. She doesn't seem interested in helping. But I've dealt with this company before, know no other, and want to get the flowers on their way, so I persevere.

We are almost done. We have gone over selection and credit card but then we hit a snag: for address, she asks - again, in a mechanical, impersonal, sing-song way - "Is this an apartment or a residence?"

An apartment or a residence?!?

Now, that's a tough question for a former English teacher, and it takes me aback. Finally, since I cannot choose between these options, I avoid it altogether and answer: "A house." But this is evidently not acceptable. She repeats: "Is this an apartment or a residence?" And I say: "I've changed my mind; I'll send candy."

I can take the lack of interest, but not the language.

A Hard Word to Say

A lovely young woman is in my speech class and, in spite of her attractiveness, she seems to be suffering from very low self-esteem. She is quite shy: she never volunteers in class and clearly struggles when she has to give a speech.

We come to the section of the course that deals specifically with language and articulation, and I mention that help is available at the speech lab. She waits for me after class and wants to know more. I encourage her to go for testing and to follow through on what they advise.

Two years later, I see her crossing the campus. She runs to greet me, takes my hand in both of hers and, with great emotion, says how grateful she is to have gotten help. She confesses that she had been afraid of college because she was ashamed of her country accent. There were many words she would not attempt because she did not know how to pronounce them and others that she thought she was saying wrong.

But a good deal of that is behind her. For example, she can now say the word, "square." And as she pronounces it, loudly, clearly, and with great confidence - "square" - tears form. Tears of pride.

Her new self is emerging.

Language liberates.

Wounded

It's the first day of high school French, and the teacher has given us a list of words. She goes around the room, asking us to pronounce when it's our turn. She calls my name, and I say, "Oih." Everyone laughs.

And the laughter stings me.

I cannot wait to get home to tell my mother because she is the very soul of kindness, and she is always on my side. "Mom, when I said, 'Oih,' everyone laughed." Mom laughs. "Honey, everyone knows that 'oui' is pronounced 'we.'"

That's when it started: the firm, deep conviction that I would never be able to speak French. I suffered through four years of it, uncomfortable every second of the way. Being called upon to speak aloud was agony. To this day, the only thing I can say in French is, "The pen of my aunt is on the table."

But I do not have an aunt. If you do, and if she speaks French, call me . . . I will tell her about her pen.

The wound of that long-ago day remains. I am ashamed to say that I have never been able to overturn that adolescent conviction.

How about you? Can you remember when a word hurt?

A Phone Call

I never do this: shop and send presents. But I happen to see just the kind of hat he has said he wants, so I get it and send it off to him at college.

The very minute he gets it, he calls to say, "I love it. Thanks so much!" He is excited and very, very pleased. So pleased, in fact, that he wants to tell me *everything*. "I never get packages, so I was surprised to see a notice in my mailbox. I hurried over to pick it up and first felt the envelope, trying to figure out what it was. It is the greatest hat; exactly the kind I wanted."

The pleasure of his words washes over me in great waves.

Later, I'm at the store and think, "What else can I buy?" I want to do this *again*.

Nothing encourages as much as words of appreciation.

Some Words Sink Deep

Flannery O'Connor's short story, "Everything That Rises Must Converge," details a complicated relationship between a son and his mother. He loves her and is tied to her with intricate, intense bonds, but he is also exasperated and infuriated by what he sees as her peculiar, old-fashioned, and stubborn ways.

I've read the story a number of times, but hadn't realized how deep its influence was.

I had a complicated relationship with my father and when my brother called to say that our father had passed away in his sleep, *as he was saying the words*, the last line of O'Connor's story flashed through my mind: (s)he entered "into the world of guilt and sorrow."

I will say no more, but am numb from what these few words have revealed.

Goals and
Hard Work

Forward Motion

I've seen dozens of charts, graphs, and statistics in my life, but numbers don't mean much to me, so I usually either don't understand them or I struggle to figure them out, only to forget everything I've learned a few days later.

But I do remember one. According to a study by the Department of Health and Human Services, for every one hundred people starting their careers in America, only 3% are financially independent by age 65.

Three percent!!! How could this possibly be?

My guess is that most people don't have goals, and without goals it is easy to drift, to lose direction. We let circumstances take over and, eventually, lose a sense of power over those circumstances.

Here is the best thing I know. I have figured it out for myself from my own drifting and have scars on my body from the cost of this insight: *the heart of self-esteem lies in a sense of forward motion.* And you cannot have a sense of forward motion unless you have a place to go *to*. So goals are every bit as essential to a healthy, full emotional and psychological life as air is to breathe.

Goals act as magnets. They draw out the person we can become.

What is drawing you?

If It Were Easy

It's early in my speaking career, so early in fact that I haven't yet decided to quit my teaching job and go into speaking full-time. The phone rings: I've been invited to Showcase at the National Speakers Association's annual Convention in July, three months from now. This is a great honor, and I am very pleased to accept.

I start thinking about the speech immediately, but it's June before I write it. The first one, that is, because I soon decide that it doesn't say what I want it to. Two weeks before the Convention, I am finally pleased with what I have and now begin to learn it. I practice out in the backyard twice a day, talking to the trees. I practice so much that soon a worn patch in the grass marks the spot of my "stage."

The Showcase finally arrives. I have spent close to eighty hours in preparation.

The Showcase is eight minutes: from 3:56 to 4:04 PM.

If it were easy, would it be worth pursuing?

Start Where You Are

I have a friend who is very talented with children. She loves young people and they, in turn, are attracted to her upbeat personality and kind, gentle ways. When her youngest was in high school, she had time on her hands, and began to think about becoming a teacher. But she did not have a college degree, and the thought of going back to college in her forties overwhelmed her. So she put aside her long-range plan and settled for a series of part-time jobs, each just a temporary stop-gap.

She made that decision fifteen years ago. She could be well into her teaching career by now but, instead, she is still doing temporary work.

I have another friend who decided when her youngest was out of college that it was now her turn. At the age of 53 she started college, finished in three years, and then went on to get her Masters in social work. She found it easy to get a job because she discovered, to her delight, that in her chosen profession, maturity was *valued*. She was a leader in her classes and continues to be one in her work. Her letters are always a delight because they are filled with the deep pleasure that comes from achievement.

It is very easy to see your goal as too far away and to give up *before you even get started.*

The trick is to look far off only long enough to identify the goal, then keep your head down and focus on one step at a time.

There is a good reason why race horses wear blinders.

Roundness

I weighed 116 pounds all through high school and college and always thought of myself as a small-boned, little person.

That little person has now become a round person. I discovered to my horror some while back that years of not-thinking-about-it had resulted in an extra twenty-five pounds. Exercise tapes came into my life. I haven't the patience to do exercises at home, but I do listen to walking tapes. Earphones in place, I head out to "make it burn."

And those folks sure do know how to motivate. They limit the exercises to doable sections and interject encouragement just when you're thinking of a Mounds Bar: "You're doing great!"; "Almost finished; keep it up now!" My favorite line is "Move it on out." With the military music blaring, I could move it on out right over to the Halls of Montezuma.

Always, about ten minutes into the routine, I think "I will do this *every* morning." And then the next morning comes and, more often than not, there is a compelling reason why I cannot walk.

But I have at least learned this: thin people deserve to be thin.

Thin is very hard work.

Progress in Stages

In 1986, when I went to my first Toastmasters meeting, I had no idea that I would someday be a professional speaker. Looking back, I can see now that Toastmasters was the start of my life's journey but, at the time, I went simply because it seemed interesting. I liked their step-by-step format and the fact that no one expected you to be good right away; the idea was simply to progress as much as you could from one speech to the next.

And we all did progress.

I was so nervous for my first speech that my notes shook and made noise. So for the second speech I improved by using notecards, but I used so many I looked as if I were ready to play canasta. By the fourth speech, I was down to one notecard and feeling proud. By speech seven, I left my notecard on the table and walked to the lectern, a distance of about six feet. But it was six miles, if measured in terms of growth and self-esteem.

Then I got a little cocky. I decided for speech ten, the all - important Speech to Inspire, to up the ante and raise the stakes: I left my notecard on the kitchen table at home, on purpose. I got into my car, started the drive to Toastmasters, and got about halfway when I had an acute anxiety attack. My palms began sweating and my heart was beating so fast that I was sure my blouse was moving. I pulled into a gas station with the idea of going home to get my notecard, but there wasn't time. I gave speech ten with no security blanket and did a terrible job. I had pushed it too far, but did learn a lesson: to this day, no matter where I speak, I have a notecard in my pocket. I never leave home without it.

Toastmasters taught me a lot, but the greatest lesson was this: progress is a process, and you can find the courage to tackle anything if you break down the task into doable, small pieces.

Take the first step, and trust that you will have what you need when the time comes for the second . . .

A Hard Worker

He appears at my office door the first week of his senior year; is applying for Law School and asks if I will write a recommendation. I am glad to do so, since he is one of the most memorable students I have ever had. The most diligent, the hardest worker.

I have written recommendations many times before; I know the requirements and tell him, now, how we should proceed. He listens politely and then says, "I have done all that already, and have brought a file for you to keep." He hands me a hanging folder with his name typed on the outside tab. Inside are three separate files, each one containing the law school's form and a stamped addressed envelope with my name and address already typed in the upper left corner. The cover sheet contains his biographical data, including dates and grade for the course he has taken with me. The recommendations are not due for another two months; he wonders if I might want the file now, or would I prefer that he come back in a month?

I am nearly speechless. I have taught for more than twenty years and have never seen such diligence.

Three years later, I am proud as we lift our glasses to toast him at his law school graduation. And if we ever need an attorney, we know one we can count on to work hard for us.

Hard work is doing the things that other people are not willing to do. And hard work pays off.

Enviable

It's 4:17 in the morning, and I wake up because I've gotten an idea for a speech I'm to give the next week. Excited, I get up to write it down before it's lost.

At 6 a.m., my husband finds me at the kitchen table and asks, "Are you going to wash the cars next?" We laugh, but we both know that I *could* wash them in record-breaking time because energy is high right now.

When work, commitment, and pleasure all become one and you reach that deep well where passion lives, nothing is impossible.

Want to achieve more? Care about what you do.

Middle Age:
The Good News

A New Phase

For the last few years I've been noticing a select few in the grocery store. They are always well-dressed, usually young, and almost always male. They carry those little shopping baskets - have you ever even touched one? - and they stand at the meat counter and point to things that cost $11/lb.

Well, guess what?!? With one child in college, and the other driving and working three nights a week as a busboy, we are *almost* there!

Seems like there are two ways to view the empty nest:
One: Sing the blues.
Two: Say, "Move over, buster. I'll have the shrimp and the lamb chops . . ."

I know my choice.

Bring it on.

Grown-Up Behavior

One of the joys of growing older is having fewer rules to follow. I'm noticing that there is now openness and flexibility among my women friends, but it certainly wasn't always like that.

As a student, didn't you feel pressure to conform? There were unwritten but important rules about the "right" clothes, the "right" groups, and the "right" behavior. And most of us stayed in line; there was very little individuality.

Although less obvious, conformity continued as a young married. I have a very clear memory of a neighbor calling one weekday afternoon and inquiring in an aggrieved tone, "I called you this morning. Where *were* you?" As if I had to report in. And, of course, instead of saying that I was free to go wherever I chose, I caved in and contritely explained my whereabouts.

But mid-life has brought relief from much of that. I have a group of women friends now whom I see only occasionally because work and separate interests keep us from getting together as a group more frequently. But when we do get together, we enjoy what we have right then, at that moment. There are no recriminations such as, "Why didn't you join us last time?" and no one keeps tabs on who is getting together separately. Each of us is free to move within or outside of the group at will.

If you get to thinking that too much time has passed since you've seen one another, you simply initiate a meeting. And if you haven't shown up in awhile, *there are no back dues to pay*; you simply appear and are welcomed.

If you don't belong to a group like this, why don't you start one?

I bet a whole lot of folks would sign up.

You Never Told Me

I'm at a Carolina Speakers Association meeting, the local chapter of NSA, and we're at the part of the program where members stand and share good news. Often people tell about an article or a book they have written or about a breakthrough in their careers.

One of our oldest members, a lady well into her seventies, stands and says, "I am angry at all of you." You can feel the shock, but we know she can't mean it because she is too sweet and she loves us too much. She must be leading up to something.

She continues: "As most of you know, I am the mother of nine children. I have been in bed a lot. But I have never been in bed, as I just was, for three months. I had a flu which took a long time to diagnose. It baffled the doctors because they said it was a youngster's disease. How could I have a youngster's disease? That was so impossible that it kept the doctors from making the correct diagnosis. But, you see, they didn't know about you. It is your fault. *You never told me I was old.*"

Doing what she loves, in the company of people she loves, has kept her young.

Do you think we could borrow her secret?

What a Relief!

It's our turn to host the neighborhood bridge group, and since a friend has just given me new recipes, I decide to try them.

The cheese dip tastes fabulous when I make it, but then I'm not sure if it should be refrigerated, which is just one of the things I hate about cooking: recipes never tell you all the little specifics you need to know. But I'm no dummy; I figure, "It's got cheese in it; it needs refrigerating."

Six hours later when our guests arrive, I pull out a two pound yellow glob and stick crackers around it. A few brave souls try, but the crackers break when you come anywhere near it and shatter if you actually make contact. "No matter," I think; folks have come for the cards and for the conversation. And, besides, we have a killer dessert.

Well, actually, I'm not sure it's a killer dessert; I've never made it, but the friend who gave me the recipe said . . .

The cards are over; everybody's now gathered in the kitchen. I get the cake; try to cut it; try to cut it; try to . . ."Don, can you cut this for me?" Another little detail: evidently the cake was also not supposed to be refrigerated.

Don gets red-faced, then close to vicious in his determination. Finally the first piece flips out, and is caught in mid-air by one of our guests.

We laugh and laugh.

But I notice that nobody finishes dessert.

A hidden blessing of mid-life: ten years ago, a mishap like this would have been a big deal.

Life Begins at . . .

OK, I confess. I love slot machines. And I knew it was time for a trip when I got change from the library's copy machine a few months ago and the sound of the coins dropping made my heart race and my palms sweat.

In the library!

So I talked my conservative husband into a trip to Las Vegas. Sin city. We saw some fabulous sights: a short, elderly man in a black shirt and white tie, a-blond-young-thing hanging onto each arm; a bride and groom in full wedding regalia at a dice table - the bride yelling, "Come on, baby!" It was all that I had hoped it would be.

But the surprise was that the town was full of retired folks. They filled the restaurants, the hotels, and the streets. They were having fun and - can you believe this? - holding hands as they walked. I thought they were supposed to be home baking chocolate chip cookies for the grandkids.

The "Golden Years" may indeed be golden.

Changing Vision

Everybody knows that your eyesight changes when you hit forty. If you haven't yet made your reading-glasses trip to the drugstore, here's how it works: the weakest prescriptions are at the bottom of the large rack, so the youngest have to bend the most. As the years progress, and as eyes regress, you move further and further up the display. If you live long enough, you can simply choose your glasses from the easy-to-reach top shelf.

Very orderly.

But eyesight changes in other ways: at weddings, for example, I used to identify with the bride. I would delight in how happy she was and study every inch of her beautiful dress.

That has changed for me; I now keep my eye on the mother of the groom. "How old do you think she is? What size is her dress? Does she look as good as the mother-of-the-bride? Does her son treat her well?"

No wonder we need new glasses; we're now looking at different things.

An Unexpected Shift

I woke up one day and realized that I have changed. For example, I used to play tennis four or five times a week, and it came as a shock to realize that I haven't picked up a racquet in at least two years. I much rather walk now and, as I walk, to think or listen to a tape or notice things. Hitting a ball has very little interest for me anymore and, for sure, I no longer care about winning . . . although I used to care very much.

This change came about so gradually that I wasn't even aware of it.

But that's just the start. In some ways, a role-reversal has taken place in our house. For years I dragged my husband to social events; now he drags me. He has a tennis group that meets once a week, and a good part of whatever socializing we do, we do because of his group.

"Do I have to go?" is still said in our house, but now it's said by a different person.

The changes go even deeper. When I quit my teaching job, some said, "You are making a mistake." The old, frightened me would have listened; the new me thought, "No, no. I believe I know what I'm doing."

And skin, I thought, got thinner as we age, but mine, thank all that is good, thickens daily. I can handle rejection and failure better now because I am learning to keep my eye focused on the inner core and my ear tuned to the inner voice.

Life is calmer.

Do you feel it too?

The Ties That Bind

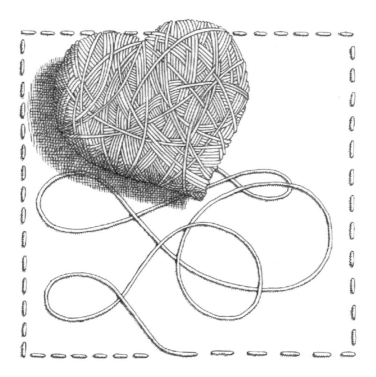

A Good Friend

My friend Cheryl doesn't let you get away with much.

On occasion, you may want to tell just part of the story, the tip of the iceberg, but she always knows when there's more. And she listens so well that before you know it, the whole thing is out, exposed. Fortunately, she is tender and trustworthy, so she treats the truth gently, safeguarding it.

Recently, we turned a two hour drive to the beach into four hours because Cheryl wanted to stop at every rest area we passed. Well, that's not true: she wanted to stop just at the first two; I wanted to stop at the others because I had learned by then the fun of getting a drink and talking while sitting under a tree. We laughed-and-cried-and-told-and-heard-secrets so intently during that drive that we needed a nap when we got to the beach. We were worn out.

By 5 P.M., revived, we were at it again, "Another thing is . . ."

What would life be like without a friend?

Magic

I remember the moment precisely.

It's late June, 1983, and we're doing errands. The boys, ages eight and five, are in the back seat and I am day-dreaming as I drive and start to fantasize about what kind of grandmother I will be. I think about how my mom used to slip the boys candy and then get defensive when caught and say, "A little bite is not going to hurt them." And the boys would grin and love it. And I would love it even though I would try not to show it.

So I day-dream that I won't start the candy habit, but that I will always bring my grandchildren something wonderful, something magical, and the cycle will continue . . . and, then, a wrenching wave of sadness washes over me because Mom has passed away and no one in this world will slip the boys a little something, "a little bite," ever again. And then I look in the rear view mirror and think: *Hold on: these boys are not grown; they are still just kids.* I turn the car around and head straight for the nearest toy store, announcing, "Boys, we are going to buy *I love you* presents."

I-love-you-presents are the greatest presents of all. They have no rules, no requirements, no timetables. They just shower down . . . like magic.

And they work even when you give them to yourself.

To See with Different Eyes

As hard as this is for me now to believe, I started college as a math major. My older brother is an engineer and was disdainful back in those early years of what he called "touchie-feelie" types. And I picked up that disdain. So I was determined when I got to college to use my mind in what I thought was the most challenging, pure, and objective way: math and science.

And I might have had a very different life if it had not been for Dr. William O'Brien, my Freshman English teacher.

He was far and away my favorite teacher, not just then but all throughout my years in school. He saw things in stories, in poems, and in plays that I never saw, no matter how carefully I had read. But once he pointed something out, I could say, "Yes. That is true." There was always layer upon layer of meaning, and I soon came to love the search and the eventual discovery. And occasionally I would catch a glimpse of something hidden, something beautiful, and he would say, "Yes. That is true." And I would glow.

So I was starting to think about changing my major to English long before the defining moment. Toward the end of the spring semester, Dr. O'Brien invited the entire class to his home for an evening book discussion. I had never seen a home like his: books everywhere, not only in floor-to-ceiling bookshelves that lined two walls of his study, but all throughout the house. Like a fabulous, cozy, friendly, good-smelling library.

Unbelievable.

And then, in the living room, a polished, ebony grand piano, which he played for us. And I heard and saw a world of beauty, comfort, and meaning that I had not known could be possible.

I have been pursuing that world ever since.

How about you? Who opened your eyes?

Mrs. Liggett

I was a baby when I went to graduate school. I shouldn't have been. I was twenty one years old, a college graduate, and a Teaching Assistant at Ohio State, teaching Freshman English as I got my Masters Degree. But I was a baby. So I was scared when I arrived, by myself, in Columbus, Ohio.

I hadn't even known to make arrangements for a place to live; I simply arrived.

After two days of looking at places I couldn't afford, I was finally taken in by Mrs. Liggett, a retired lady who lived across the street from the Law School and who, against her better judgement, allowed me to rent her extra bedroom.

Our relationship began very formally. She had heard lots of stories about wild graduate students, about late nights and parties, and she wanted no part of it. She made that very clear. But by the time of the first snow, we were friends and we would sometimes sit for hours as she told stories from her youth.

Many were about Charlie, the husband who had left her forty

years before. Charlie cared a lot about food, and his young bride didn't know how to cook. As soon as Charlie would leave for work, she would make dinner. Then, when it was awful - as it almost always was - she would bury it in the backyard and start over again.

I can still picture a backyard studded with mounds of buried string beans and meatloaf. And I can certainly still picture Mrs. Liggett and all her many kindnesses.

I wrote to her for years, at first at the Columbus address and later at a nursing home. In time, she stopped answering; then, one awful day, my letter was returned marked "undeliverable."

I hope she's in a great place now where she doesn't have to cook and – if she wants – she has Charlie at her side.

She Shines Her Light

A friend lends me a tape of an interview with a nationally recognized speaker, someone I have heard about for years. I'm in bed when I listen, in the dark . . . with earphones, so it's not just listening; it's more like mainlining. And her words sink into my bloodstream. Even though it's 2 A.M., I get up and write to her.

And she answers.

She says, "*Yes.*"

And that, "*Yes,*" resonates for me, and gives me courage. I might not have written this book without her insight: I wrote and asked, "How to start? . . . seems overwhelming." And she answered, "Forget the word 'overwhelming.' Overwhelming is having kids when you never did before. And preparing dinner for thirty-five years. And working <u>and</u> cleaning house while you're broke! And we *still* did it. It has been ready for forty years, waiting. Write the book, Nancy."

Once, after confessing deep, heart-rendering troubles and doubts, and baring my soul, her reply began, "Listen, pal, let me set you straight."

No, no. You listen, pal. You have set me straight . . . in ways too many to count.

Rosita Perez, you shine your light, and we advance toward its glow.

A Good Man

My friend Gesine told me about the humor test when we were in college. Her family had a living room chair with a broken back leg; you would rock dangerously and could sit comfortably only if balanced just right. When a date would call for Gesine, her dad would say, "Have a seat, young man," and point to *the chair*. Then Dad would watch. If the young man were too self-conscious to mention his predicament, he would fail the test. But if he were open about it, and if he laughed, then Dad would later say, "That's a fine young man."

I had forgotten about the test until years later, when Don and I were in the getting-to-know-you stage and telling our stories. Don talked about his first summer away from home. He had gotten a job at Yellowstone National Park and went to California for the long July 4th weekend. He had dreamed of Malibu; of surfing. He saw himself, a transplanted Mid-Westerner, carrying his board, wearing shades, flipping his hair back, California style.

But here's what really happened: he got the board all right, but his arms weren't long enough to hold it at his side. He had to carry it with two hands, flat-out-in-front-of-him. "Picture this," he said, as he described himself struggling along the famous beach.

And I could picture it.

We laughed and laughed. Suddenly I remembered Gesine's Dad and his conviction that a sense of humor is the most important ingredient in a lasting marriage.

And then I laughed from joy . . . and from the magic of discovery.

Mom

Our first child is about six months old when Mom and Dad come for a visit and Mom is as excited about him as I had hoped she would be. She declares him "the greatest baby I have ever seen" and never tires of hearing about his accomplishments. In fact, she encourages me to keep talking.

I have been hungry for this and bask in her love and praise.

The next morning, he is on a blanket in the middle of the living room floor, contentedly holding his bottle and drinking apple juice. As doting and devoted as I am as his mother, I pay no attention since I've seen this dozens of times. But my mother thinks it is beyond adorable. She calls my father, who is in the kitchen content with his newspaper. "Dave, Dave, come quick." He rushes in. They both look down; my mother's face is the very picture of grandmotherly pride, "Have you *ever* seen anyone drink apple juice like that?"

My heart moves inside my chest. A twinge, a jolt.

For that moment, and for many more like it, I love her beyond words.

The Bottom Line:

*The real prizes are always **inside**.*

THE BOOK MAY BE FINISHED, BUT THE MESSAGE IS NOT!

LOOKING FOR A SPEAKER FOR YOUR NEXT MEETING?

The reviews are in. . .

Turn the page to read evaluations of Nancy Coey's programs.

WANT TO GIVE GIFTS TO YOUR FRIENDS?

See the last page for an order form.

WHAT OTHERS ARE SAYING ABOUT NANCY'S KEYNOTES AND SEMINARS . . .

"Absolutely WONDERFUL luncheon speech; what a difference YOU made in our meeting."

Community Action

"She re-taught me to look for the good in students."
"Dynamite! She was perfectly placed after lunch . . . no one could even <u>think</u> of sleeping!"
"I wish my colleagues had gone to this talk!"

School System

"Perfectly tailored for the audience and directly on target!"

Child Support Council

"A winner! You made the Professional Development Committee look good!"

Utility Company

"She used real life situations, and brought the audience of 1600 to their feet with a standing ovation."

School District

"Sweetcakes."

Smart-aleck teenage son

"Rave reviews . . . we will certainly use Nancy's talents again."

Association Executives

"Informative, warm, and humorous presentation. Your examples and stories were so realistic and down-to-earth each of us could relate."

Nurses Association

"Thought-provoking, soul penetrating, sincerely delivered. Thank you, Nancy, for giving of yourself."

School Administrators

"Outstanding! Your ability to relate to your audiences is exceptional. You provide stories that are based on life experiences that everyone can find a common link with. Powerful!"

Professional Saleswomen

"Wonderful! Entertaining and intimate."

Government Meeting Planners

"You were the best part of the conference! The poem you wrote will be treasured and become a classic!"

Extension Service

"She touched my heart and soul."
"Made you hang on to every word."
"Kept the crowd laughing."
"Very good at motivating listeners; also very entertaining."
"She should write a book!"

Women's Conference

CELEBRATE!

HAVE NANCY COEY SPEAK
AT YOUR NEXT MEETING

For information about Nancy's programs, contact:

Nancy Coey
4705 Twinwood Court
Raleigh, NC 27613-6115
919-848-9743

Give GIFTS to Your Friends . . .

Mail Order To:
Sweetwater Press
PO Box 68124
Raleigh, NC 27613

Please send me _____ copies of
Finding Gifts in Everyday Life @ $11.95   Total $_____
(For personalized copies, please include names.)

North Carolina residents: add 6%
sales tax ($.71 per book) $_____

Add $2.50 first book; $.75 each additional,
for shipping and handling $_____

Enclosed is check or money order
PAYABLE TO SWEETWATER PRESS   **TOTAL:** $_____

Send To:

Name _____

Address _____ Apt. #_____

City _____State _____

Phone (___) _____Zip Code _____

Fax: 919-848-9784   Phone : 919-848-9743